W9-CFH-355

Numbers

Written by Jennifer Dryden
Illustrations by Steve Mack

FlashKids

New York

FlashKids

New York

An Imprint of Sterling Publishing
387 Park Avenue South
New York, NY 10016

FLASH KIDS and the distinctive Flash Kids logo are trademarks of Barnes and Noble, Inc.

© 2011 by Flash Kids
Illustrations © 2011 by Flash Kids

All rights reserved. No part of this publication may be reproduced, stored in a retrieval system, or transmitted,
in any form or by any means, electronic, mechanical, photocopying, recording, or otherwise,
without prior written permission from the publisher.

ISBN 978-1-4114-5810-9 (paperback)

Distributed in Canada by Sterling Publishing
c/o Canadian Manda Group, 165 Dufferin Street
Toronto, Ontario, Canada M6K 3H6
Distributed in the United Kingdom by GMC Distribution Services
Castle Place, 166 High Street, Lewes, East Sussex, England BN7 1XU
Distributed in Australia by Capricorn Link (Australia) Pty. Ltd.
P.O. Box 704, Windsor, NSW 2756, Australia

For information about custom editions, special sales, and premium and corporate purchases, please contact
Sterling Special Sales at 800-805-5489 or specialsales@sterlingpublishing.com.

Manufactured in Canada
Lot #:
2 4 6 8 10 9 7 5 3 1
11/11

www.flashkids.com

Dear Parent,

Numbers offers simple and complex activities that progress from writing numerals and number words to simple counting activities, including connect the dots and hidden picture activities. As you work through this book with your child, offer guidance on difficult activities, but allow your preschooler to work through challenges independently. When the workbook is complete, reward your child with the certificate provided on page 79. **For free downloads and fun activity ideas, visit www.flashkids.com.**

Have your child make an "L" shape with his or her pointer finger and thumb. Lay the pencil at the crease of the "L" shape, allowing the tip of the pencil to rest on the middle finger. Ask your child to pinch his or her pointer finger and thumb to the pencil so it is comfortable. Begin writing! Reinforce the proper way to hold a pencil if your child is having trouble.

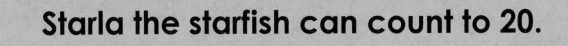

Starla the starfish can count to 20.

1 2 3

4 5 6

7 8 9

10 11 12

Soon you will, too!

13 14 15

16 17 18

19

20

Trace the number I.

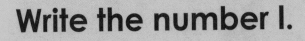

Write the number I.

Starla wants to make I new friend.
Color I fish.

Trace the word one.

one one one one one

Write the word one.

Count the clownfish below.
Then circle the group that shows one.

Trace the number 2.

2   2   2   2   2

Write the number 2.

Starla likes to ride on the side of a sailboat.
Color 2 sailboats.

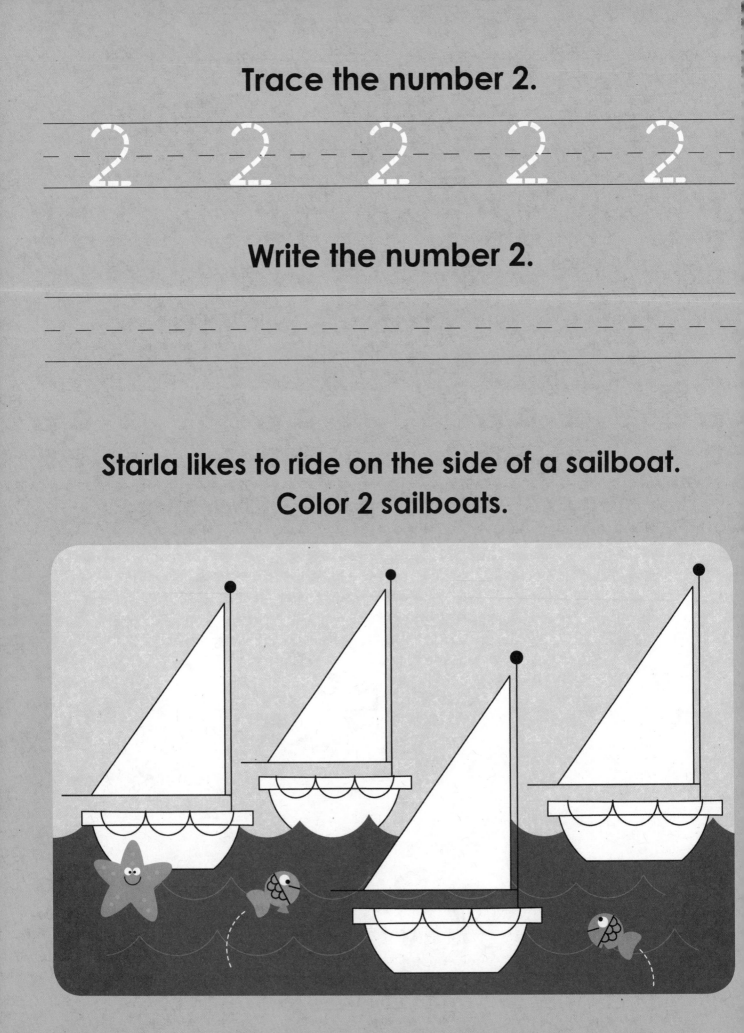

Trace the word two.

two two two

Write the word two.

Count the sailboats below.
Then circle the group that shows two.

Trace the number 3.

3 — 3 — 3 — 3 — 3

Write the number 3.

Waves bump the kids up and down.
Color 3 rafts.

Trace the word three.

three three three

Write the word three.

Count the rafts below.
Then circle the group that shows three.

Trace the number 4.

4 — — 4 — — 4 — — 4 — — 4

Write the number 4.

It is lunch time. Yum!
Color 4 picnic baskets.

Trace the word four.

four   four   four

Write the word four.

Count the sandwiches below.
Then circle the group that shows four.

Trace the number 5.

5   5   5   5   5

Write the number 5.

Starla finds five more friends.
Color 5 crabs.

Trace the word five.

five   five   five

Write the word five.

Count the crabs below.
Then circle the group that shows five.

Trace the number 6.

6   6   6   6   6

Write the number 6.

Wear a sun hat to keep cool in the hot sun. Color 6 sun hats.

Trace the word six.

six   six   six

Write the word six.

Count the sun hats below.
Then circle the group that shows six.

Trace the number 7.

7 7 7 7 7

Write the number 7.

Starla likes to swim with her starfish family.
Color 7 starfish.

Trace the word seven.

seven   seven   seven

Write the word seven.

Count the starfish below.
Then circle the group that shows seven.

Trace the number 8.

8   8   8   8   8

Write the number 8.

There is a sand toy shaped like Starla the starfish! Color 8 sand toys.

Trace the word eight.

eight   eight   eight

Write the word eight.

Count the sand toys below.
Then circle the group that shows eight.

Trace the number 9.

9 - - 9 - - 9 - - 9 - - 9

Write the number 9.

- - - - - - - - - - -

Palm trees sway in the breeze.
Color 9 palm trees.

Trace the word nine.

nine   nine   nine

Write the word nine.

Count the palm trees below.
Then circle the group that shows nine.

Trace the number 10.

10 - - 10 - - 10 - - 10

Write the number 10.

- - - - - - - - - -

Starla likes to surf!
Color 10 surfboards.

Trace the word ten.

ten   ten   ten

Write the word ten.

Count the surfboards below.
Then circle the group that shows ten.

Trace the number 11.

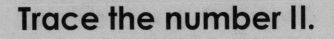

Write the number 11.

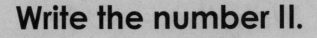

Fish swim in groups called schools.
Color 11 fish.

Trace the word eleven.

eleven   eleven

Write the word eleven.

Count the fish below.
Then circle the group that shows eleven.

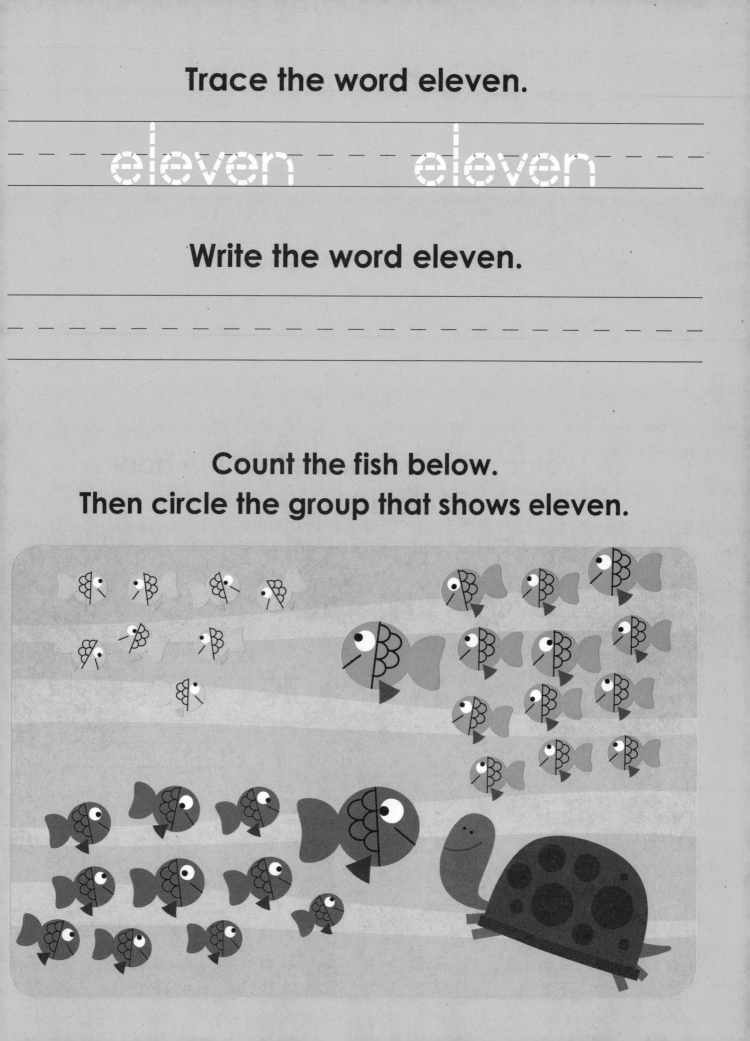

Trace the number 12.

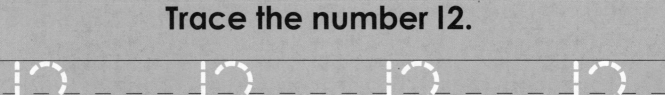

12   12   12   12

Write the number 12.

A woman reads Starla's favorite book.
Color 12 books.

Trace the word twelve.

twelve   twelve

Write the word twelve.

Count the books below.
Then circle the group that shows twelve.

Trace the number 13.

13 - - - 13 - - - 13 - - - 13

Write the number 13.

Starla finds clams with pearls inside!
Color 13 clams.

Trace the word thirteen.

thirteen   thirteen

Write the word thirteen.

Count the clams below.
Then circle the group that shows thirteen.

Trace the number 14.

14   14   14   14

Write the number 14.

It is fun to play catch!
Color 14 beach balls.

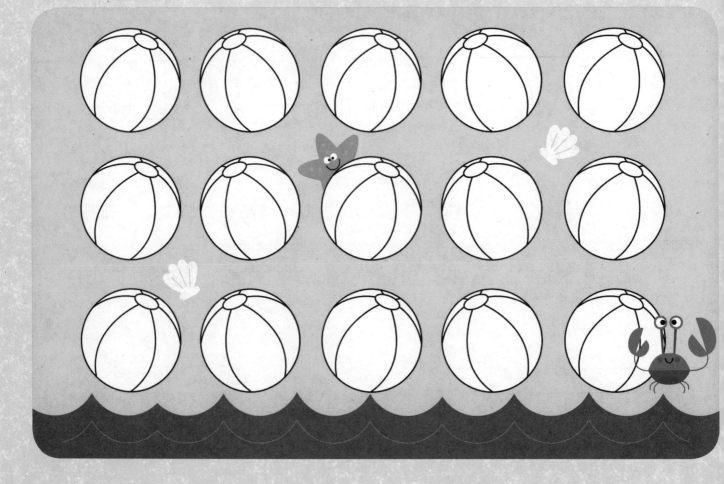

Trace the word fourteen.

fourteen   fourteen

Write the word fourteen.

Count the beach balls below.
Then circle the group that shows fourteen.

Trace the number 15.

15   15   15   15

Write the number 15.

It is a sea of sea horses!
Color 15 sea horses.

Trace the word fifteen.

fifteen   fifteen

Write the word fifteen.

Count the sea horses below.
Then circle the group that shows fifteen.

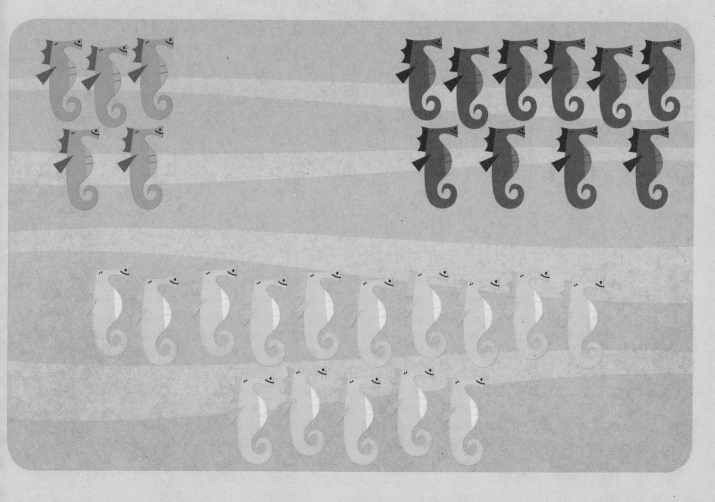

Trace the number 16.

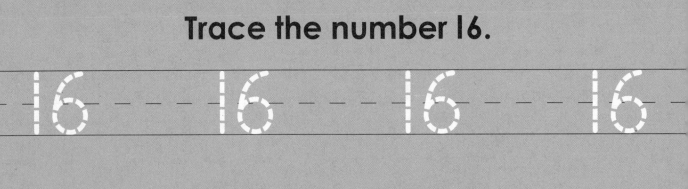

16 - - 16 - - 16 - - 16

Write the number 16.

The polka-dotted octopus is Starla's teacher. Color 16 octopus arms.

Trace the word sixteen.

sixteen   sixteen

Write the word sixteen.

Count the octopus arms below.
Then circle the group that shows sixteen.

Trace the number 17.

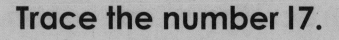

Write the number 17.

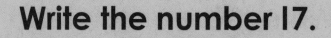

The kids fly kites on the beach.
Color 17 bows.

Trace the word seventeen.

seventeen   seventeen

Write the word seventeen.

Count the kite bows below.
Then circle the group that shows seventeen.

Trace the number 18.

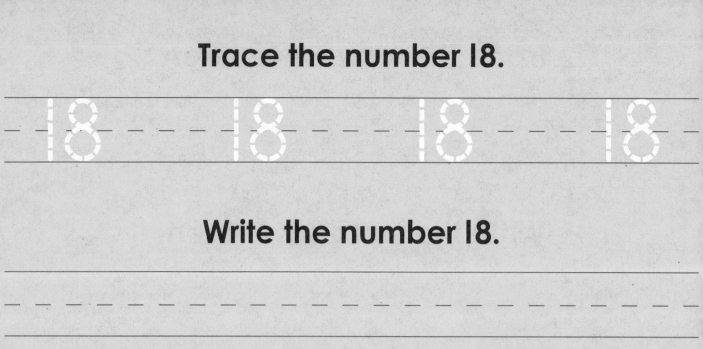

Write the number 18.

A submarine sinks down. Bubbles float up. Color 18 bubbles.

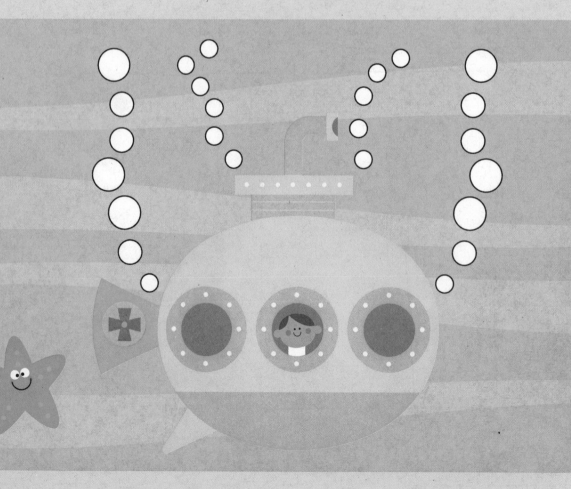

Trace the word eighteen.

eighteen   eighteen

Write the word eighteen.

Count the bubbles below.
Then circle the group that shows eighteen.

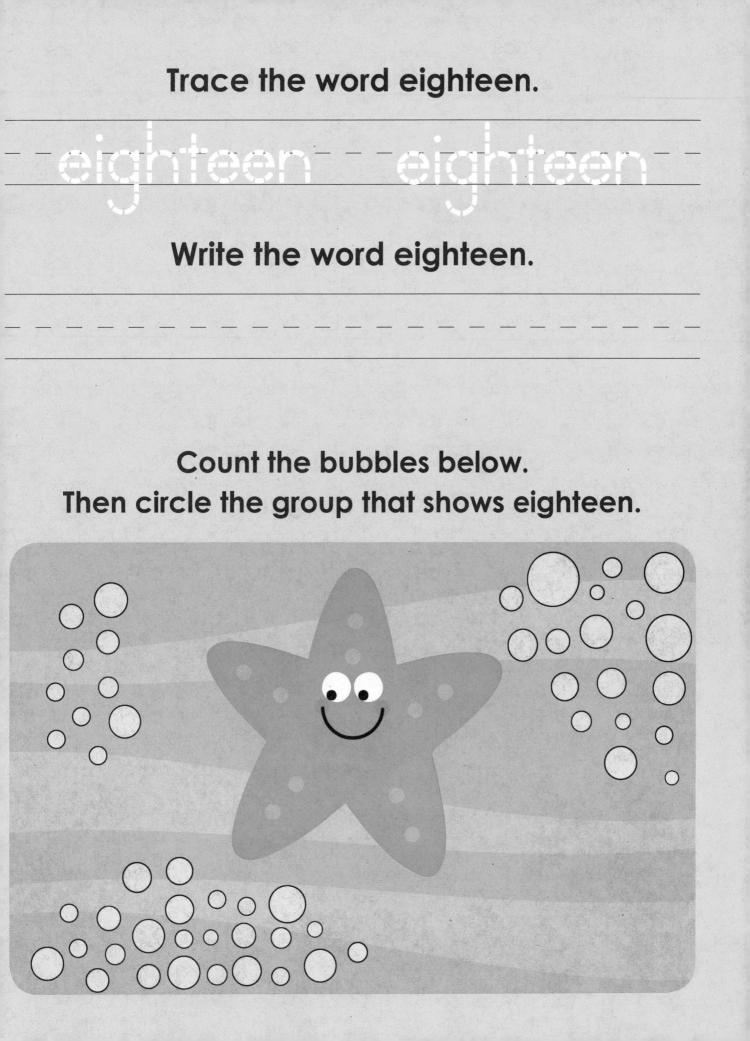

Trace the number 19.

19   19   19   19

Write the number 19.

Seagulls look for fish in the water.
Color 19 seagulls.

Trace the word nineteen.

nineteen   nineteen

Write the word nineteen.

Count the seagulls below.
Then circle the group that shows nineteen.

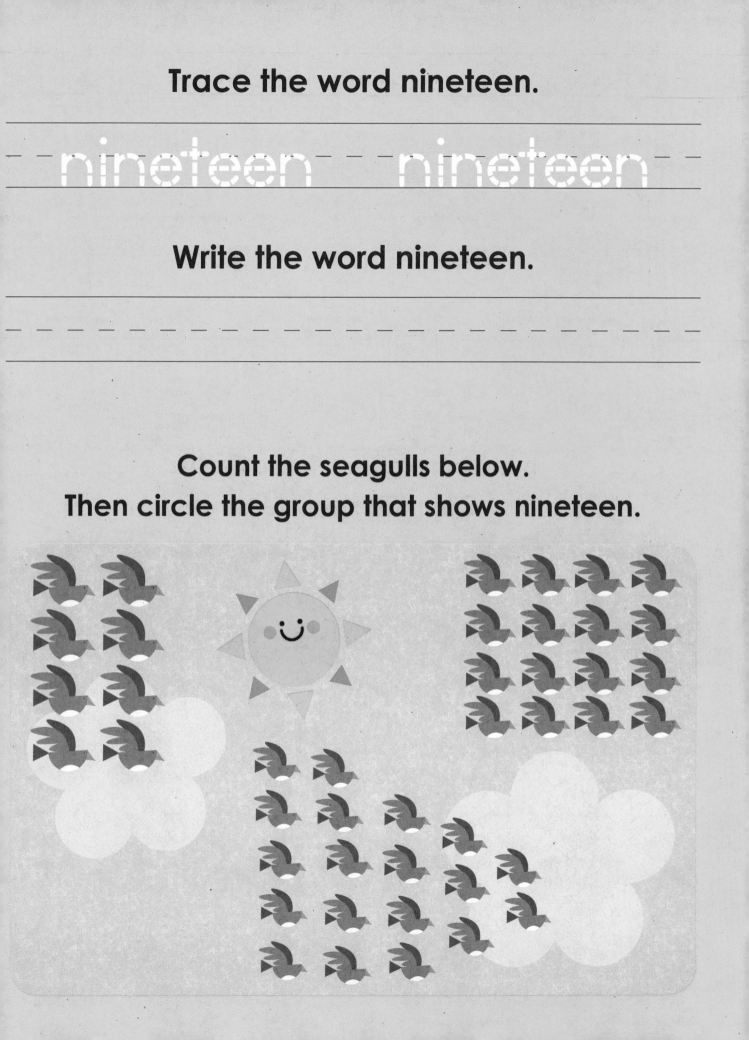

Trace the number 20.

20 - - 20 - - 20 - - 20

Write the number 20.

It is fun to collect seashells.
Color 20 seashells.

Trace the word twenty.

twenty   twenty

Write the word twenty.

Count the seashells below.
Then circle the group that shows twenty.

Help the baby sea turtles crawl from the nest to the ocean. Connect the numbers from 1 to 5.

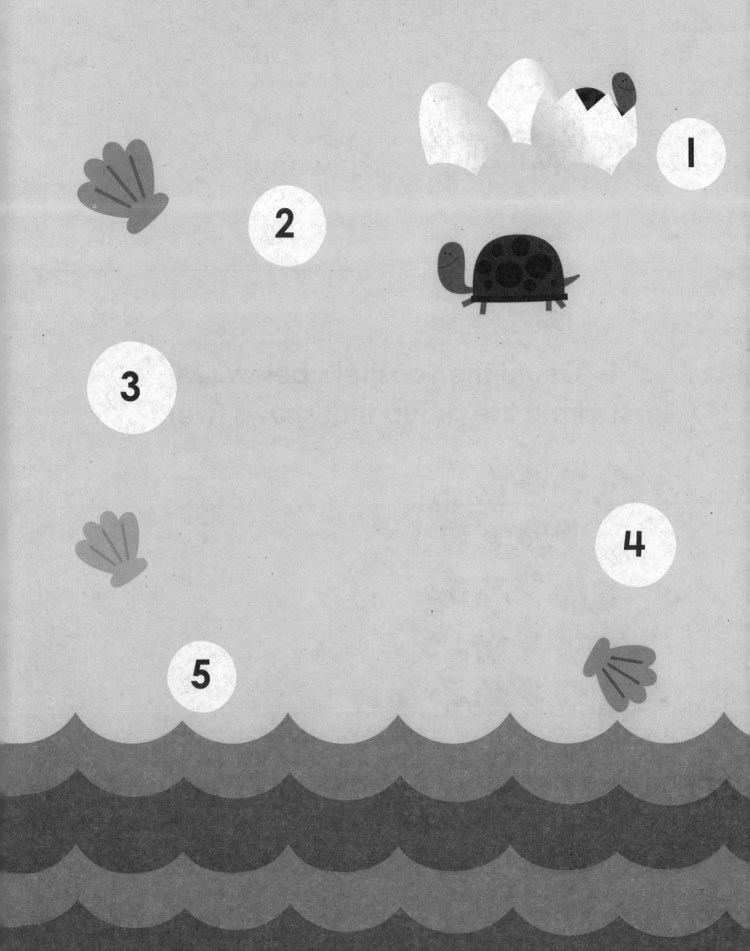

The lifeguard works to keep you safe at the beach or pool. Find and circle the hidden objects from the clues below.

1   1   2   3

Which underwater creature has electricity in it?
Connect the dots from I to 5 to find out.

Look at the picture below.
Count how many of each object you see.
Write the number on the line next to the object.

What animal jumps high above the water?
Connect the dots from 1 to 5 to find out.

Airplanes write messages in the sky.
Find and circle the hidden objects from the clues below.

Have a nice day!

1   2   3   4

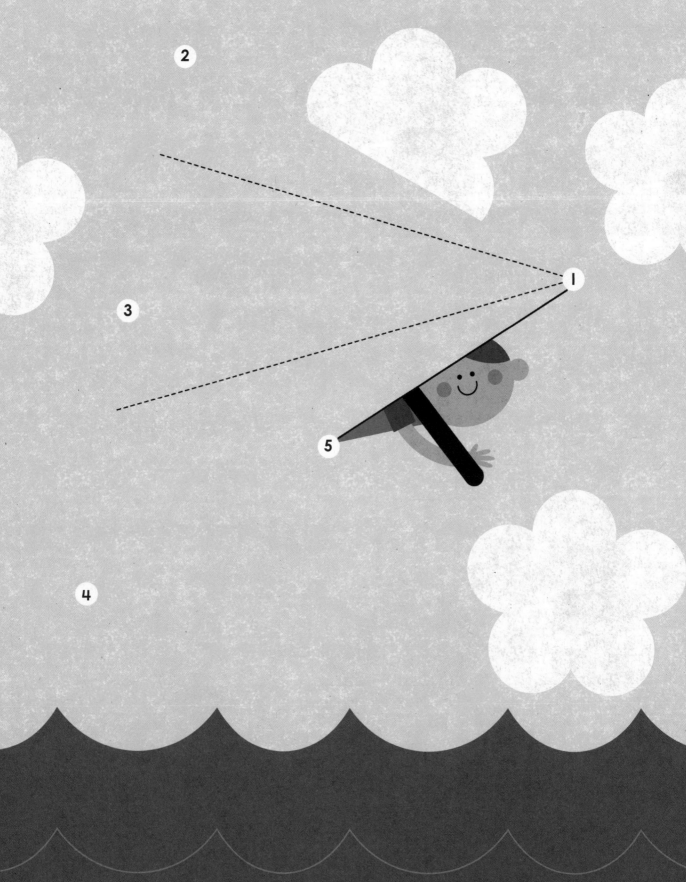

Look at the picture below.
Count how many of each object you see.
Write the number on the line next to the object.

_____   _____   _____

Help the sun warm the ocean water.
Connect the numbers from I to IO.

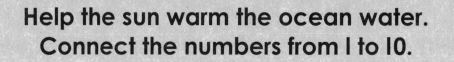

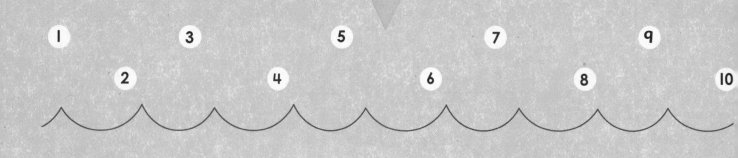

1   3   5   7   9

2   4   6   8   10

So many creatures live in the ocean!
Find and circle the hidden objects from the clues below.

1

3

4

10

How can Starla protect her eyes from the bright sun?
Connect the dots from 1 to 10 to find out.

Look at the picture below.
Count how many of each object you see.
Write the number on the line next to the object.

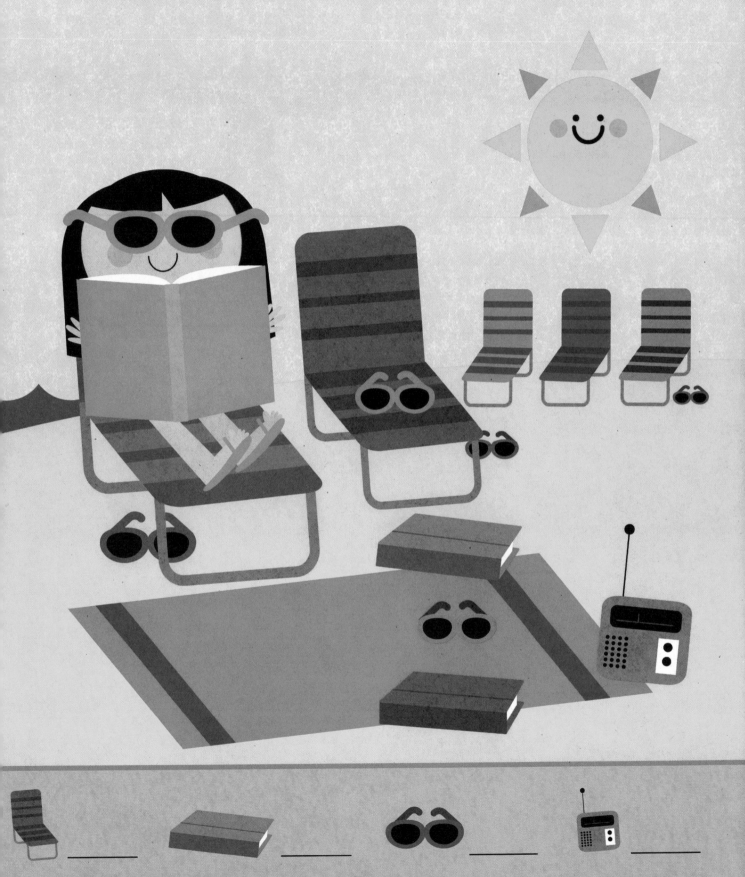

Where do surfers ride their surfboards?
Connect the dots from 1 to 10 to find out.

3

4

5

6

7

2

8

9

10

1

So many creatures live in the ocean!
Find and circle the hidden objects from the clues below.

2   3   4   5   10

How can Starla cool down on a hot day?
Connect the dots from 1 to 10 to find out.

Look at the picture below.
Count how many of each object you see.
Write the number on the line next to the object.

Boats race on the water.
Connect the numbers from 1 to 10.

Trace the crab's trail.
Connect the numbers from 1 to 15.

How do sailors find their way in the dark night?
Connect the dots from 1 to 15 to find out.

Look at the picture below.
Count how many of each object you see.
Write the number on the line next to the object.

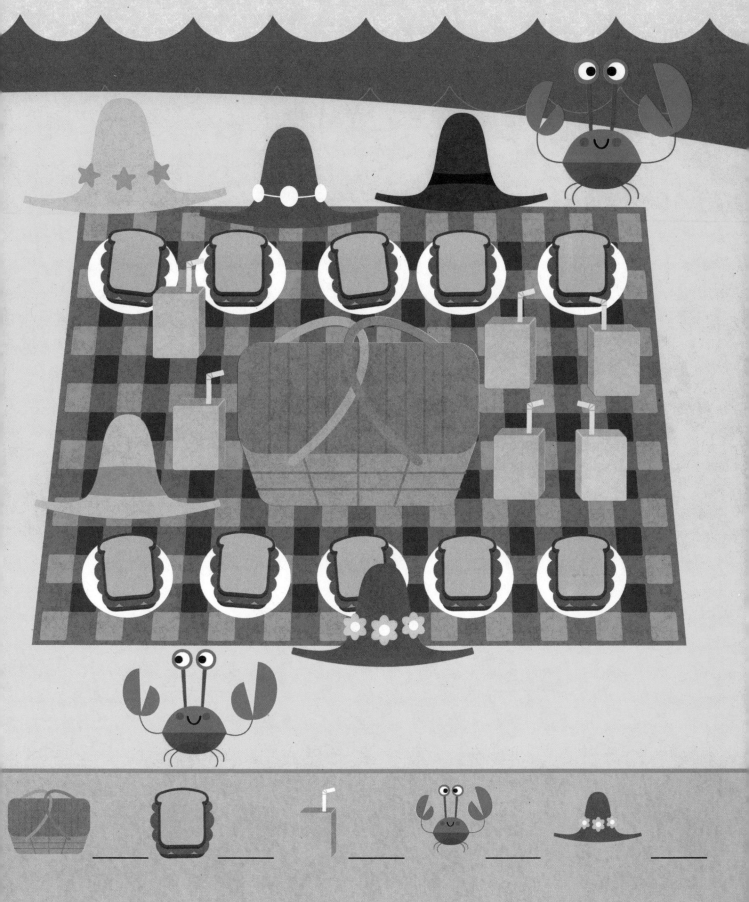

_____   _____   _____   _____   _____

What beach sport are the kids playing?
Connect the dots from 1 to 15 to find out.

Look at the picture below.
Count how many of each footprint you see.
Write the number on the line next to the print.

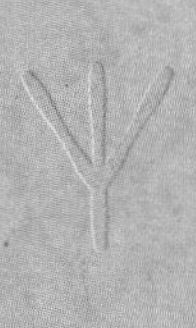

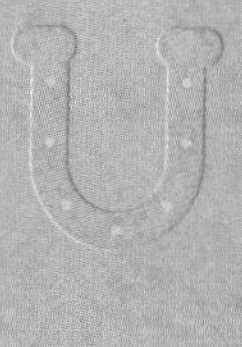

Y _____   ⫎ _____   U _____

What keeps a boat from floating away?
Connect the dots from 1 to 20 to find out.

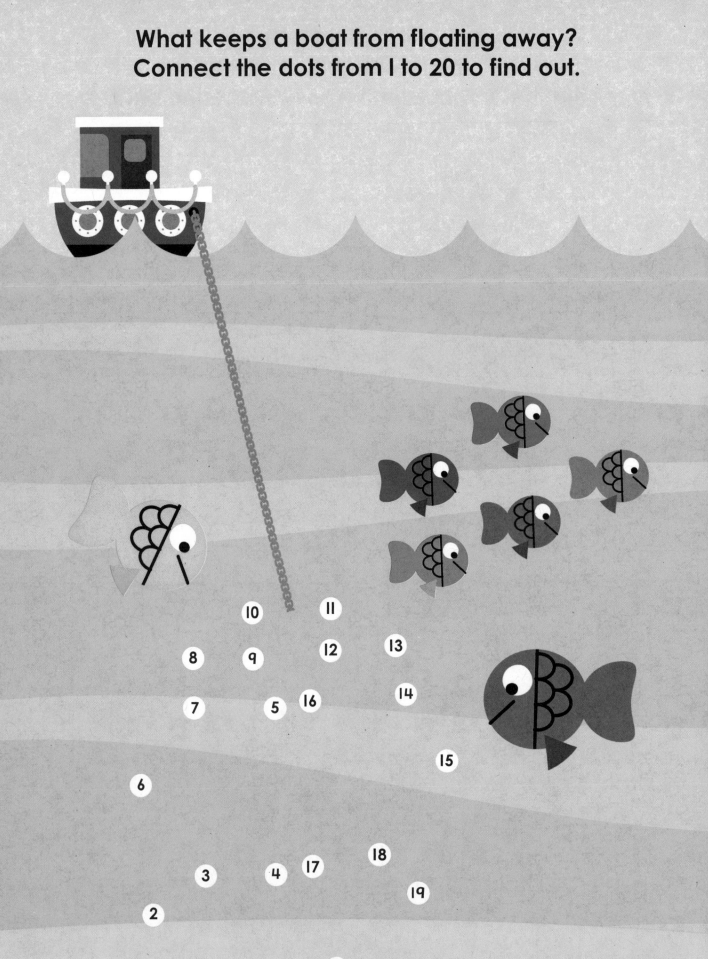

Look at the picture below.
Count how many of each object you see.
Write the number on the line next to the object.

What kind of boat takes people on vacation?
Connect the dots from 1 to 20 to find out.

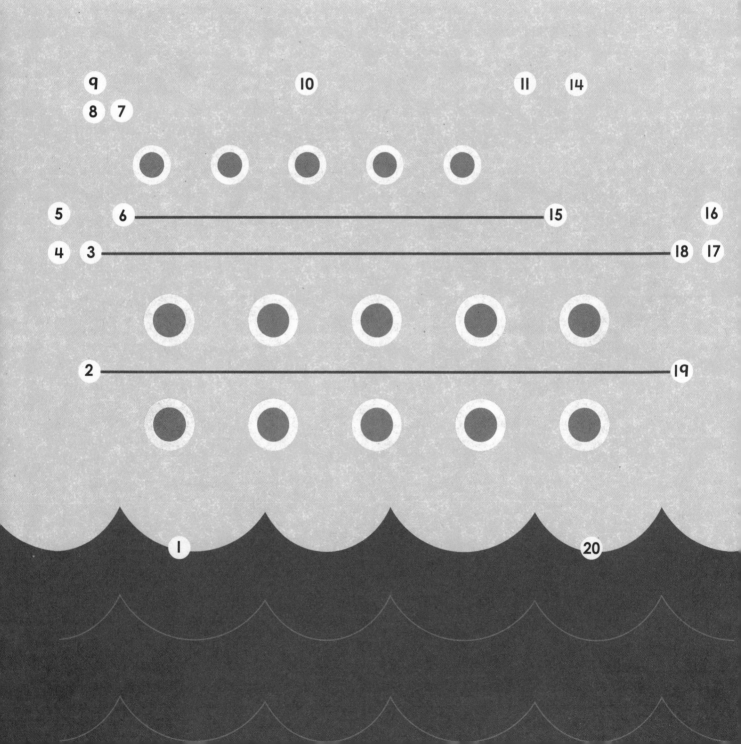

Snorkeling lets you see life underwater!
Find and circle the hidden objects from the clues below.

2   **8**   **10**   **13**   **17**

Where can you find some shade at the beach?
Connect the dots from 1 to 20 to find out.

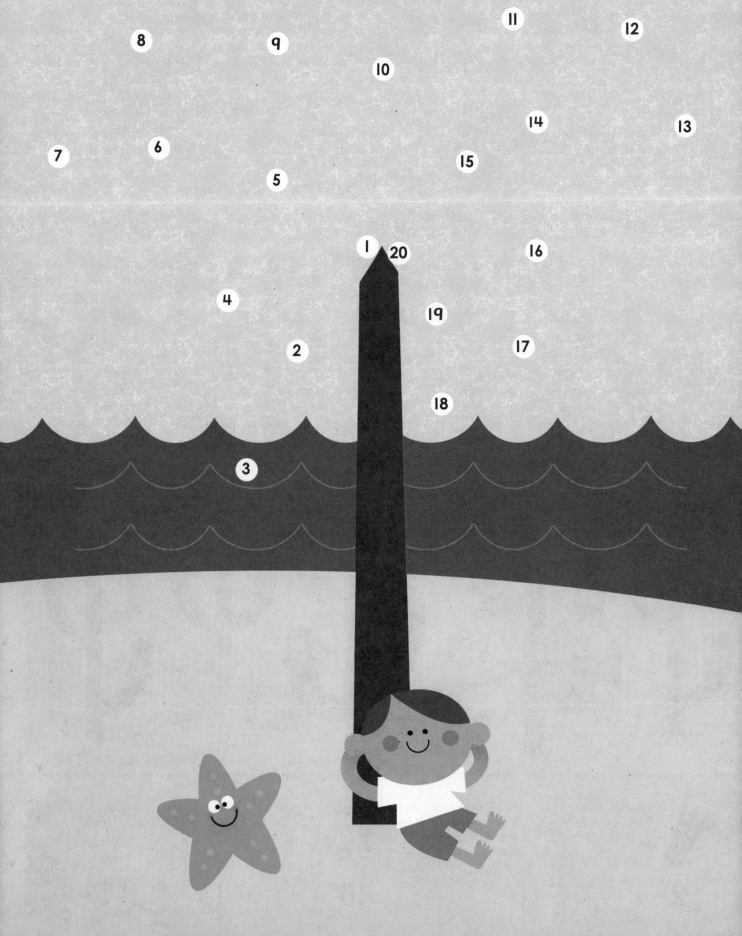

Look at the picture below.
Count how many of each object you see.
Write the number on the line next to the object.

Where do these fish like to swim?
Connect the dots from 1 to 20 to find out.

It is fun to build sandcastles!
Find and circle the hidden objects from the clues below.

| 1 | 3 | 5 | 8 | 10 | 20 |

What underwater creature has eight arms?
Connect the dots from 1 to 20 to find out.

Look at the picture below.
Count how many of each object you see.
Write the number on the line next to the object.

_____   _____   _____   _____   _____

Help Starla practice counting all of her beach friends. Connect the numbers from 1 to 20.

Congratulations!

has successfully completed
Numbers.